The Incredible 5-Point Scale

Assisting students with autism spectrum disorders in understanding social interactions and controlling their emotional responses

Kari Dunn Buron and Mitzi Curtis
2 teachers from Minnesota

The Incredible 5-Point Scale

Assisting students with
autism spectrum disorders
in understanding social interactions
and controlling their emotional responses

Kari Dunn Buron and Mitzi Curtis
2 teachers from Minnesota

Autism Asperger Publishing Company
P.O. Box 23173
Shawnee Mission, Kansas 66283-0173
www.asperger.net

©2003 by Autism Asperger Publishing Co.
Reprinted 2004
P.O. Box 23173
Shawnee Mission, Kansas 66283-0173
www.asperger.net

Publisher's Cataloging-in-Publication
(provided by Quality Books, Inc.)

Buron, Kari Dunn
    The Incredible 5-point scale : assisting students
with autism spectrum disorders in understanding social
interactions and controlling their emotional responses /
Kari Dunn Buron and Mitzi Curtis.
    p. cm.
    Includes bibliographical references.
    ISBN: 1-931282-52-8
    Library of Congress Control Number: 2003114610

    1. Autistic children–Rehabilitation. 2. Autistic
children–Education. 3. Autism in children. 4. Social
skills in children. I. Curtis, Mitzi II. Title.

RJ506.A9B87 2003   616.89'82
                          QBI03-200501

This book is designed in Century Old Style and Elvenfont

Managing Editor: Kirsten McBride
Interior Design and Production: Tappan Design and Eddy Mora

Printed in the United States of America

This book is dedicated to our
wonderful families, who not only
support our passions,
but encourage and nurture them!

Contents

Introduction

We are two special education teachers working in the public schools in the Twin Cities area of Minnesota. We have over 20 years of classroom experience and are currently working as autism resource specialists, supporting students with autism spectrum disorders (ASD) and their teachers within the classroom. We also teach at Hamline University (St. Paul, Minnesota) in the ASD certificate program for special educators. We are particularly interested in the social cognitive disorder present in ASD and in helping students understand where and why social interactions sometimes fall apart.

Problems related to lack of social competence and understanding of one's own impact on a social interaction receive little attention in teacher preparation programs. Kanner (1943) and Asperger (1944) discussed social dysfunction as a central part of autism and Asperger Syndrome, respectively, but that fact is often ignored in educational programs in this country. Addressing problems of social understanding can be confusing for teachers and parents because we are only just beginning to understand their impact on the development and prognosis of people with ASD.

The objective of this book is to illustrate how to utilize a simple 5-point scale to support a program for teaching social understanding. There is nothing new about scales. We have all read about 5-point scales and 10-point scales – scales that look like thermometers and scales that look like a volume control on a stereo. We have used scales for years to help students rate their anger, feelings, or pain. However, one day while problem solving with a student and his teacher, Theresa Urmann, regarding the student's voice volume, we had an epiphany – a major "a-ha" moment. Not only did this student respond positively to rating volume on a 1-5 point scale (and this student was otherwise not known for responding positively to many interventions!), he also participated in assigning the point values and specifying where it is OK and where it is not OK to use a particular voice. He later asked his teacher to help him by reminding him of which number his voice should be at. From then on the student and Theresa began to "talk in numbers" rather than in socially and emotionally laden words. All of this made sense, given what we know about ASD – the scales are visual and they reduce abstract ideas to simple numbers, thus matching some of the major learning characteristics of students with ASD.

Admittedly, we excite easily, but this was *really* fun. We began listening to descriptions of challenging behavior with the 5-point scale in mind. We tried the scales with kindergarten students with autism and with teenagers with Asperger Syndrome. During this process, we came dangerously close to believing that every social concept and social behavior can be neatly explained, examined, and analyzed by reducing it to a 5-point scale! Quite frankly, we began to see 5-point scales everywhere.

We found that the 5-point scale was particularly successful with students with Asperger Syndrome, but it also worked well with students with ASD who had some social readiness skills, such as attending, and who could identify numbers or colors. We also found that it was best introduced in a 1:1 teaching session. Once the student understood the ratings, the scales could be used in small groups both at school and at home. We began to accumulate scale success stories from a variety of students. We even bought special high-priced colored markers to make more and more visually appealing scales!

Sometimes writing a story to go with the scale was a successful way to introduce the purpose of the scale and clearly outline how the scale works. These stories took the form of a "memo" or simply a written description of the problem. The idea of using a story as a way to give students clear, concrete social information came from Gray's (1995) work on social stories. Social stories are stories written in a very specific way using sentences that describe social situations, state the perspectives of the people involved, and gently give direction to the person with ASD. They were originally designed to give students with ASD more information about a social event or misunderstanding.

It is our hope that this book will give you ideas about how to break down a variety of behaviors into concrete parts to help your student or child better understand what it is you are asking of him. You do not need high-priced colored markers to start (unless you are as obsessive as Kari is!). Simply rate the behavior from 1-5 and *write it down*. Sometimes "**5**" is seen as a positive direction, sometimes it is seen as a lack of control. We have found that it does not seem to matter which direction you choose. The idea is to break down a concept, so the top or bottom of each scale may not necessarily represent good or bad. For example, not talking may not be a good thing all the time, but if you are breaking down volume, a "**1**" may need to represent no talking because that is the lowest possible volume and a "**5**" may represent screaming for help, which is the highest volume but may not be a good thing if used in the classroom. Ideally, you want the child or student to help you define each number, but this is not always possible. We have found that filling in the number values for the person can also be effective.

Between the two of us, we work with a great variety of students. We have seen the scale work positively with students who have multiple labels, including autism, Aperger Syndrome, Tourette Syndrome, attention deficit hyperactivity disorder, obsessive compulsive disorder, and oppositional defiant disorder. The idea is that how we act, react, and interact in difficult situations depends on our ability to quickly and efficiently assess what is happening and consider the consequences of our actions. Students who lack social competence can benefit when repetitive problems are broken down into clear, concrete parts. Hopefully, we have given enough examples to be helpful to everyone who works with or lives with a person who lacks such social competence.

Enjoy!
Kari and Mitzi

A "5" Means I Am Screaming

Ned is a kindergarten student with Asperger Syndrome and obsessive compulsive disorder. He just couldn't understand about voice volume in the classroom. He loved to scream just for the fun of it, and often talked in a really loud voice. If you said, "Ned, you need to talk softly," he would respond, **"Why are you saying that!"** (in a very loud voice).

We decided to compare volume to big and little and put it on a 5-point scale. The results were not immediate, and it took a lot of patience on the part of Ned's kindergarten teacher to keep working on it, but eventually Ned was able to recognize when his voice was too loud. To help prompt him, all the adults at school carried small 1-5 point scales in their ID tags. When Ned's voice got too loud, the adult would take out the scale and point to the volume he should be at.

At first this bothered Ned, and he would scream, "Don't show me a 2!" The adults were instructed not to respond to such outbursts, but to simply point to the number as a nonverbal prompt. Over time, Ned began to respond positively. The following story also helped Ned to "study" the concept.

When my voice gets too big

When no words come out of my mouth, my voice is at a **1**.

When my teacher is talking to me, I should try to keep my voice at a **1**. *No talking at all.*

Sometimes my voice is little.

Some people call this a **soft voice**.

This is when my voice is at a **2**.

I use a **2** voice when I am in the library. A **2** is like a whisper.

My teacher would like for me to try really hard to keep my voice at a **3** in the classroom.

This is like when I am talking on the phone or talking to my friends at lunch or asking the teacher a question.

When I get upset, my voice might go to a **4**. This is when my teacher can remind me about using a **3** or **2** voice in school.

If I am out at recess and I want someone to throw me the ball, I may have to use a **4** voice to get their attention.

A **4** voice is pretty loud and I should try not to use a **4** in school or in a building at all. A **4** is sometimes called an outside voice.

Maybe a **4** could be used if I am at a ball game and I am rooting for my team.

A **5** means I am screaming.

I should only use a 5 if it is an emergency and I am calling for help. I should try to never use a **5** unless it is a real emergency.

It is important to know about how loud my voice is.

Some places actually have rules about how loud your voice can be, and all kids have to learn about voices.

My teachers can help me remember about my voice by pointing to the number on the scale it should be at.

They don't even have to talk about it. They can just point to the number and then I will know that I accidentally got too loud.

5 Emergencies

4 Outside; at a ball game

3 In the classroom; at lunch

2 In the library; quiet time

1 When someone else is talking at the movies

Voice Scale

 **5** Screaming / emergency only

_____

 **4** Recess / outside voice

_____

 **3** Classroom voice / talking

_____

 **2** Soft voice / whisper

_____

 **1** No talking at all

When Words Hurt

Joey has Asperger Syndrome; he is in the third grade. He is very bright and likes to share his special interest in the Civil War with his teacher and classmates. Joey is fully included in the third grade and does well, with one exception: He upsets other children and his teacher when he says mean and hurtful things.

Joey often yells at other students when they say something that bothers him. Sometimes he is rude to others and calls them names. Not surprisingly, this hinders Joey's ability to make or keep friends. In fact, some of his classmates are afraid of him, and this is upsetting to Joey.

Joey thought that the only reason someone should be upset with him was if he actually hit or kicked the person. He thought it was illogical to get mad at words because words cannot cause bodily damage. One thing that has helped Joey understand the impact his words have on other people is a 5-point scale that illustrates various degrees of interaction. We used the scale to help explain the degrees of social interactions to him.

For example, he got very upset with a student who was sitting next to him and yelled, "Will you be ignorant forever!?" This was upsetting to the other student, who asked to be moved to the other side of the room. Joey was very upset by the student's response to his behavior. He couldn't understand why telling the truth would make her mad.

We explained it using the 5-point scale, with 4 and 5 behaviors being very upsetting to others. We also drew a cartoon to illustrate the social situation – with Joey yelling at the other student and the other student thinking, "Joey's behavior is at a 4. Those words hurt and make me want to move as far away from him as I can. Those words make me a little afraid of Joey because sometimes people who say mean things also do mean things." Joey asked if he could keep the cartoon in his desk and often studied it. We wrote a story about how words hurt to help clarify this concept for Joey.

There is no question that Joey is still confused by others' reactions to his words, but he is beginning to accept the fact that other people sometimes think differently than he does. Below is a copy of the cartoon that helped Joey understand the rating scale.

When Words Hurt – A Story for Joey

Sometimes other people say and do things that make me mad.

Sometimes they give the wrong answer in class or break a rule, like cutting in line.

When people do these things, I get frustrated and before I think things through, I say things that are very mean.

When I was little, I used to kick people when they said or did things that made me mad, so I figured words were better than kicking.

Actually, words are better than kicking, but words can still be scary and hurtful.

When I say hurtful or mean things, other people may *think* I want to hurt them or that I don't like them.

When I say mean things, other people might decide to not be my friend any more.

My teacher can try to help by defining #4 words for me. I can write those words on my scale and try to remember not to use them when I am mad.

I can also keep a journal of the things that make me mad. Sometimes writing it down gives me just enough time to think about not using those #4 words.

The Touching and Talking Scale

 Punching/kicking

_____

 Being mean (saying mean things)

_____

 Talking in a friendly way

_____

 Looking in a friendly way

_____

 Thinking in a friendly way

The Obsessional Index

Kevin is in the fifth grade. He has Asperger Syndrome and obsessive compulsive disorder. Kevin is obsessed with balls and will go to great lengths to find a ball and then throw it on top of the highest available ledge or roof. The ball-throwing obsession becomes a problem when he hurts others to get at a ball or when he runs through the school with a ball trying to find a high ledge. His anxiety over ball throwing is so intense that his thinking becomes illogical.

The following is Kevin's account of his ball obsession, which he reported to his teacher when she interviewed him as a part of a functional behavior assessment:

"I don't want to be obsessed with balls or balloons. It is a stupid obsession. I can't be the boss of anything. I want to be back to being a baby again. Maybe then I could start over. When I go to people's houses, I steal their balls, and that's embarrassing. No one in the neighborhood understands me. I hate obsessions. They make me mad. I really want to get rid of them but I can't. I can't do anything right. Every time I see a ball, I have to have it. I know right from wrong but this is just too hard."

The 5-point scale was designed to teach Kevin how to recognize his need for support in dealing with his obsessions before it was too late. On some days, he didn't even seem to think about balls; in fact, on those days his obsessive personality seemed to help him to stay focused on his work. On other days, he would think about balls but it didn't seem to bother him much. On those days, he was so relaxed that he could handle thoughts about balls.

Some days he just wanted to talk about his obsession with balls. If the adult with him told him not to talk about it, it often led to increased anxiety and acting-out behavior. Some days Kevin would come off the bus already talking rapidly about balls, types of balls, sizes of balls, and so on. We knew that on those days, he was going to need added support. This support often meant that Kevin did his work outside of the classroom to lower his anxiety about "blowing it" in front of the other kids.

Kevin had refused social stories in the past because he thought they were for "babies." Instead, we wrote him a memo to explain the new scale idea. Kevin loved the memo and kept it with him. He checked in with the special education teacher each morning to rate himself, and within a month he was accurately rating his anxiety about balls.

After we introduced the memo to him, there have only been a few days when Kevin had to work outside of the classroom for most of the day because his anxiety was high. Although he continues to have occasional rough days, he has not had to leave the classroom since we started the program.

MEMO

MEMO

To: Kevin

Re: When Your Obsessions Get Too Big

Sometimes having obsessions can be a positive thing, because it means that your brain is capable of latching on to an idea and not letting go. This can be beneficial for great explorers, inventors and writers. BUT sometimes having obsessions can be very upsetting and frustrating.

This memo is to inform you that I understand that sometimes your obsessions get so big that you are not able to control them because of the severe level of anxiety they cause. It would be highly beneficial for you to learn to tell the difference between when your obsessions are too big to handle and when they are feeling more like positive obsessions. One way to do this is to do a "check-in" three times a day when you consider your obsessional index. The first step is to help me fill out the following chart by rating your obsessional index on a 1-5 rating scale. Thank you for your cooperation.

Kari Dunn Buron

Obsessional Index

 I can't control it. I will need lots of support.

 I am feeling very nervous and will probably need some support.

 I am thinking about my obsessions, but I may need to talk to someone about it. I think I have some control.

 I am feeling pretty relaxed today. I can probably think about my obsessions but still do well in the classroom.

 It is a great day! My obsessional personality is a neurological work of art!

The Incredible Home Scale

The home scale was created for Lindsay, a 10-year-old girl who has autism. She tends to get anxious and stressed away from home, at the swimming pool, grocery store, church, and so on. As a result, when given a direction by her parents, she often screamed, kicked, and hit as a first response. This behavior was consistent whether the environment was unpleasant or exciting.

Lindsay's mother began teaching her daughter to rate herself on a 5-point scale: (a) before they left the house, (b) when they arrived at the destination but before leaving the car, and (c) then periodically while they were at the event or place. Finally, Lindsay's parents would have her rate herself prior to letting her know it was time to leave. This helped in preparing her for the transition to come.

Since it was important for her parents to honor Lindsay's rating, they carried small pads of paper so they could easily give her visual directives, such as writing out "Let's take a walk" when she had rated herself at a 3 and did not want anyone to talk to her. When she rated herself at a 4, her parents silently walked out to the car, and typically Lindsay followed to get away from what was upsetting her.

On those occasions when she didn't follow, Lindsay's parents felt that they had waited too long and that she had entered a 5 status. When Lindsay was at a 5, it was too late to move gracefully. Sometimes her parents opted to physically move her, but it was usually more prudent to just give her space. Giving her physical space often helped to calm her down, but touching her when she was already highly stressed usually resulted in uncontrolled aggressive behavior such as scratching and biting.

As Lindsay's parents learned to recognize subtle signs of stress, they prompted her to do a rating so that they could teach her to connect the subtle signs of stress with a 2 or a 3 rating. The long-term goal was for Lindsay to recognize those early signs of stress and excuse herself from a given situation.

Lindsay's parents learned that some environments were too stressful for her, and had to make some tough but more realistic decisions about their own expectations. For example, they wanted to take Lindsay with them to church, but realized that the environmental demands of church were too stressful for her and therefore made arrangements for Lindsey to stay at home.

When I Go Out

I love being at home.

I especially love my bedroom and the family room because all of my stuff is there.

Our schedule usually stays the same at home, so I almost always know what is going to happen.

Sometimes I go out with my parents.

Going out can be fun, but it can also be stressful.

One place I like to go is the YWCA.

I love to swim when I go to the Y.

When it is time to get out of the pool, it is often hard for me because I love it so much.

I don't want my parents to tell me to get out of the pool.

Another place we go is church. I don't like going to church.

I have to sit still for about an hour and that is too hard.

Sometimes I make noises and that bothers my mom. She keeps telling me to be quiet, and sometimes I scream out, "You be quiet!"

Yikes! The other people at church have a hard time listening when I yell like that.

My mom and dad get pretty upset when I yell at church.

One way to try and make things better when we go out is for me to learn more about how I feel and how to tell my mom and dad how I feel. That way they can help me when I start to lose control.

When I am doing something I really like (like swimming), I am usually at a **1**. This means I am handling it just great!

But my **1** can go to a **2** really fast if my mom tells me it is time to leave and I don't want to. When I am at a **2**, I am getting a little nervous.

When I am at a **3**, I usually scream things like "shut up!" I can let my mom and dad know about being at a **3**, and they will know that I need for them to stop talking right now.

Sometimes I am at a **3** for the whole visit, like when I am at church or when we go to my Uncle Ed and Aunt Sally's house.

I can let my mom and dad know that it is hard for me to be some place by telling them that I am at a **3**. If I am at a **3**, they can take me for a short walk.

When I get really nervous, I am at a **4**.

When I am at a **4**, it is important for me to go to the car.

My mom and dad always have special activities for me in the car (they are in my car bag). These might be my Little Mermaid figures, my squish ball, or my Gameboy.

When I am at a **4**, I need to think about relaxing. Closing my eyes and rubbing my legs and arms helps me to relax.

I should always let my mom and dad know before I go to the car. For example, I can yell out "4!" and they will know.

I can try really hard to bring my **4** down to a **3** by playing with my relaxing car activities.

I can handle **3**'s much better.

Sometimes everything falls apart, and I need my mom and dad to help me calm down by taking deep breaths, not talking, and standing two arm's lengths away.

This is when I am at a **5**.

When I am at a **5**, I sometimes hurt other people and don't even know it.

I need lots of help when I am at a **5**. I usually need to take a nap after I hit **5**.

Keeping myself at a **2** is my goal. The more I work on this, the easier it will be!

The Incredible Home Scale

 **5** I need to leave!

_____

 **4** I need some space

_____

 **3** Please don't talk

_____

 **2** I am a little nervous

_____

 **1** I can handle this!

22

Meeting and Greeting Others

Alex is in the first grade. He has Asperger Syndrome and is fully integrated in regular education classes with support. He wants to have friends but has difficulty approaching other kids appropriately. He often hits or kicks other students and gets into trouble. When questioned about this behavior, he denies ever hitting or says the other student deserved it because he was being ignored and that should be against the rules!

Recess is Alex's hardest time because it is loud on the playground and there is so much fast movement going on. He often gets very frustrated when he cannot get another student's attention. The following is a story written for Alex to introduce his 1-5 point scale as a way to help him control his frustration and approach students in a socially acceptable way.

Helping Alex Meet Friends

I really like to talk to other kids.

Sometimes on the playground I try to talk to other kids but they don't listen.

I get so frustrated when this happens.

Sometimes I say mean things or pull on their clothes to get them to look at me.

When I say mean things or pull on clothes, the other kids say they don't want to be near me.

I need to remember to only use 2 and 3 behaviors when trying to talk to my friends.

2 and 3 behaviors are friendly words and friendly faces.

My teacher can help me by letting the other kids know I am trying really hard!

Meeting and Greeting Others Scale

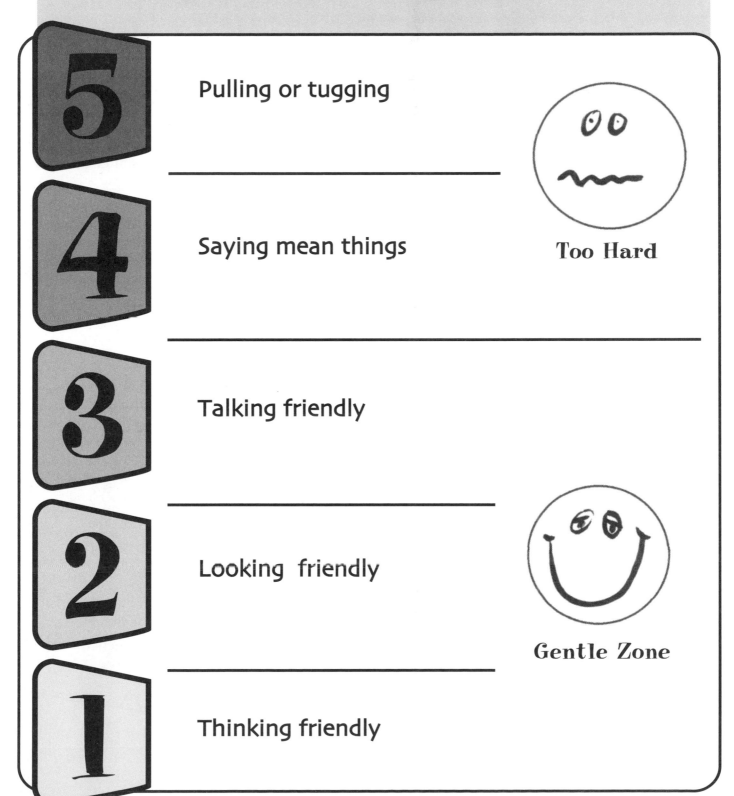

5	Pulling or tugging	
4	Saying mean things	Too Hard
3	Talking friendly	
2	Looking friendly	Gentle Zone
1	Thinking friendly	

Control This!

Colton is in the fourth grade. He has Asperger Syndrome and has had problems getting along in school since he was in kindergarten. He likes to be in control and gets upset if he perceives that something is "wrong." For example, if someone cuts in line he may feel compelled to punish that person by kicking or hitting him.

Curiously, Colton's ability to control his aggressive response to others' behavior seems to vary greatly from day to day. One day he may not be bothered by another student taking two milks at lunch. The next day the same offense may be too much for him to handle and he may end up kicking the offending child. Colton's mother does not work outside the home, so she is able to come to the school and pick him up when he becomes aggressive.

The team decided to help Colton by using a 1-5 point scale to teach him to recognize his own ability to "control" his reactions. Using the scale, he started to check in with the principal four times a day to rate his level of control. If he rated himself at a 4, he would have an alternative recess (like playing chess with the principal) and eat lunch in the classroom with a friend rather than in the less structured and noisy cafeteria. If he rated himself at a 5, he would call his mother, who would come to pick him up before he lost control.

This program would not work if Colton did not like school, but he loved school, so he did not rate himself at a 5 very often. He was also very rigid and did not like to stay home because that meant a change in his day. He enjoyed recess and liked playing hockey, so he didn't rate himself a 4 unless he was very close to getting into trouble.

The program has not eliminated Colton's aggressive behavior, but it has helped him understand his lack of control. It has also helped the team realize that he needed more supervision and support in large social settings.

Learning About Control

Control is a funny thing. It helps to learn more about it and about myself.

It's okay to want to be in control. Being in control can make you feel more relaxed about things.

Sometimes I have lots of control. I am relaxed and feeling good.

I call this being at a 1.

Sometimes I have some pretty good control. I can usually make a good choice when I have pretty good control.

I call this being at a 2.

Sometimes I don't feel great. I may not even want to be at school. Maybe I just don't feel like talking.

On these days I don't have really good control.

I call this being at a 3.

Sometimes I get up on the wrong side of the bed!

I am grumpy on those days and may not be able to make very good choices.

I wouldn't call this very good control – in fact, I almost don't have any control.

I call this being at a 4.

Then there are those really, really bad days.

They don't happen very often but when they do, look out!

Sometimes I just lose all control.

I can't make good choices and sometimes I am in danger of hurting someone else.

This is being at a 5.

It is good to learn about control so I can learn to be more independent, successful, and capable!

Name: _Colton_   My _Control_ Scale

Rating	Looks like	Feels like	I can *try* to
5	Kicking or hitting	My head will probably explode	Call my mom go home
4	Screaming at people <u>Almost</u> hitting	Nervous	Go to see Mr. Peterson
3	Quiet sometimes rude talk	Bad mood grumpy	Stay away from kids (The ones I don't like!)
2	Regular kid - <u>not</u> weird!	Good	Enjoy it while it lasts
1	Playing hockey	A million bucks $	Stay that way!

What I Really Meant Was . . .

Emily is a fifth-grade student with Asperger Syndrome and Tourette Syndrome. She goes to a special school for students with severe behavior challenges. The program typically uses positive programming, but if the staff feel a student is becoming aggressive, a forced timeout – the stop-and-think room – may be implemented. Emily often complains that she has to sit in the stop-and-think room for not doing her work. Emily's teacher insists that she never goes to the stop-and-think room for noncompliance, only for threatening behavior.

We were asked to help create a program for Emily that would help her understand the perspective of others and the impact her behavior has on others, including her teacher. After observing Emily during a typical struggle with her teacher, we decided to meet with Emily and her teacher to discuss perspective-taking using a 5-point scale.

Emily truly did think she was getting in trouble for not doing her work. What seemed to be happening was the following.

When Emily refused to do her work, her teacher responded with an angry posture (her face and her body). When Emily perceived her teacher as being angry, she became defensive and engaged in verbally challenging behavior. If her teacher responded verbally to her challenges, Emily would start yelling. Often the yelling escalated to swearing and insulting remarks. At this point, Emily's teacher interpreted her behavior as one step before explosive and therefore directed her to the stop-and-think room. All the while, Emily did not feel she was out of control.

To problem solve this situation we first used a 5-point scale to define Emily's control, with 5 meaning out of control. Emily told us that if she was hitting, she was at a 5 but that if she was running out of the room, she was only at a 4. She said that she was hardly ever mad when she swore, so that was rated a 3.

When we interviewed Emily's teacher, she agreed that hitting was a 5. However, she thought that Emily's swearing was a 4 because it felt angry and intimidating. She agreed that Emily was probably still in control when she was just rude but not swearing.

We put the two scales side by side to illustrate the two different perspectives. We then drew a curve to visually illustrate Emily's level of anxiety. We used the scale to explain to Emily that her teacher had to predict when Emily would get out of control so that she could protect herself and the other students. We put the teacher's 1-5 ratings on the curve to help Emily understand that her teacher's actions were based on how she thought about what she was seeing and hearing.

The teacher and Emily agreed to try to "talk in numbers" in the future. The teacher agreed that if Emily swore, she would ask her what number she was at. If Emily said that she was at a 3, the teacher agreed to walk away and give her time to cool down. Emily also made cards with the numbers 1-5 on them and agreed to try to give the teacher a card when she was upset, instead of talking rudely.

The program had a dramatic effect on improving Emily's behavior as well as her relationship with her teacher, who became a wonderful advocate for Emily when the team began to plan for middle school.

Emily's Perspective

 **5**   I hit at other people

_____

 **4**   I run out of the room

_____

 **3**   Sometimes I swear

_____

 **2**   I'm quiet but mad and tense

_____

 **1**   I'm feeling OK about things

Emily's Anxiety Curve

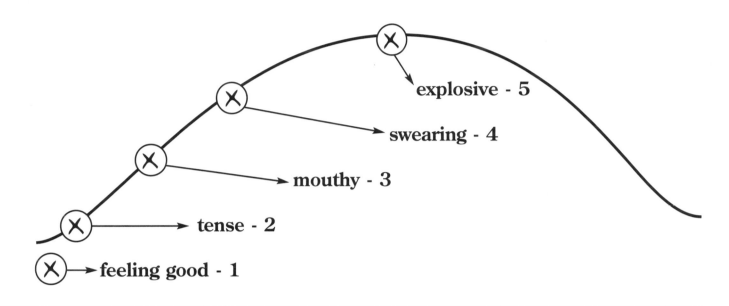

	Emily thinks	Mrs. Olson thinks
5	hitting	hitting
4	running out of the room	swearing
3	swearing	mouthy
2	mad/tense	challenging
1	ok	working

Emily goes to the stop-and-think room when Mrs. Olson *thinks* she is close to an explosion.

Meagan's Touching Scale

Meagan is a seventh-grader with autism. She has recently begun developing physically and has started touching her breasts at school. The school team felt that she was trying to get attention because she often touched her breasts and then looked at her teacher for a reaction. This behavior was particularly problematic when Meagan was in the general education settings such as homeroom or lunch. Peers often became so uncomfortable with her behavior that they would move away. It seemed the more her teacher asked her not to touch herself, the more Meagan would do it.

First, we introduced some touching rules to Meagan through a social story (Gray, 1995). We discussed the approach with Meagan's parents to be sure we were in agreement about what to say and how to define the different levels of touch.

The school team agreed to read the story to Meagan each morning and to post her scale in her work area as a reminder. In addition, Meagan's teacher wore a small 1-5 point scale (see Appendix) around her neck with her ID tag to prompt Meagan nonverbally when she touched her breasts. The teacher was instructed by us to touch the 2 on her scale to prompt Meagan to bring her 5 touch down to a 2.

Meagan's inappropriate touching behavior at school decreased by 40% within the first month of this new program. Besides, Meagan's parents reported that the scale was being used successfully at home. Her parents added a red 5 card to prompt Meagan to go to her bedroom when they began to get a sense that her touching was becoming inappropriate.

Touching Rules

I can touch my arms or legs or even my breasts.

It is important to learn about when I should touch my body and when I should not.

It is important to remember my touching rules.

I like to touch myself.

I like to watch other people's faces when I touch myself.

But here's the deal:

Some people feel uncomfortable when I touch myself in certain places of my body.

We can call that touch a 4 or a 5.

Some people do not want to sit next to someone who touches themselves at a 4 or 5.

I need to try really hard to remember about the touching rules.

I can read my touching story every day to help me remember.

My teacher can post my touching scale in my office to help me remember.

If I forget, my teacher can point to a 1 or a 2 on her little scale so that I can try to change my touching level.

I can be really *cool* and follow the touching rule.

The Incredible 5-Point Scale

Name: Meagan   My Touching   Scale

Rating	Touch what?	Where can I do it?
5	Breasts Genitals	Bedroom - Door closed
4	Thighs Bottom Inside nose	Bedroom or bathroom
3	Bare feet Belly	At home
2	Arms Legs Hair	Anywhere
1	No touching	Anywhere

When Using a Quiet Voice Isn't Necessarily a Good Thing

Larry is an 11-year-old boy with ASD who is very soft-spoken. He often waits for the prompt, "What do you need Larry?" before he asks.

The following scale was Larry's first use of a number- and color-combined rating scale.

For Larry, the topic of voice volume was perfect. His social skills group had been working on filling in the colors and numbers on the scale. We then assigned a voice volume to 5, deciding that 5 would be yelling. After preparing the group for what was about to happen and covering our ears, the facilitator demonstrated yelling. As you can imagine, the kids thought this was pretty funny. We then defined 1 as not talking at all. We practiced having our mouths closed and open. We practiced not talking. Level 2 was identified as whispering, and then we practiced whispering. Number 3 on the scale was defined as conversation, and we practiced talking so that our partner could hear us but not the entire group. Finally, we decided that 4 would just be loud, which might mean the person we were talking to would have to back away a bit when we talked. We also practiced that.

Larry, as well as many of the students in the group, seemed to need more than just the numbers, words, and practice to fully understand the concept of voice volume, so we added color and faces. This particularly helped Larry as he struggles with reading and number concepts and has difficulty discriminating between colors. Many students with ASD could benefit from using multiple visual cues (colors, numbers, pictures) to explain the concepts defined by their scales.

As Larry was coloring his scale, he stopped when he came to the number 5. He needed a red crayon but he did not ask. The teacher prompted him, and he whispered "Crayon, please." The facilitator pointed to the 2 and said, "Larry, you said 'crayon, please' at a 2. To get Wilma's (educational assistant with the crayons) attention, try saying it at a 3." He did, and promptly got the red crayon.

After about 10 more minutes of rating voice volumes with numbers and colors, a new teacher came into the room. Larry wanted to tell her that he wanted to check his schedule. Without offering any other prompt, except pointing to the 4, Larry said in a very 4 voice across the room, "Diane, excuse me, check schedule, please." Diane responded with, "Okay, bring it over to me and we'll check." In the past, Larry would have whispered his request and then waited for someone to prompt him to initiate the interaction with Diane. The scale worked!

Voice Volume for Larry

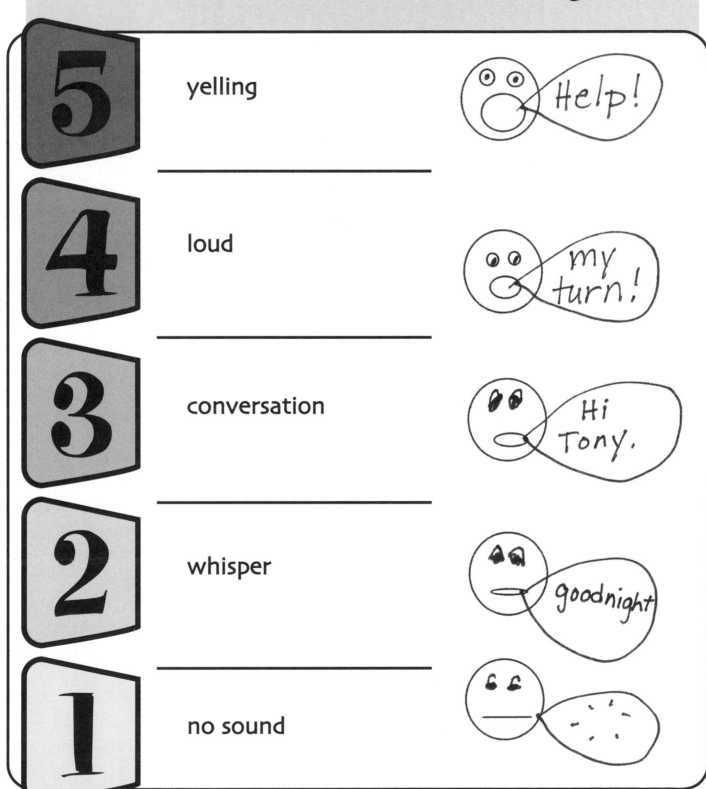

5 — yelling

4 — loud

3 — conversation

2 — whisper

1 — no sound

It Even Works with the Big Guys

The following rating scales were developed with and for young men with Asperger Syndrome attending a special high school for students with behavior challenges. We began working with these students one on one with their teacher present so that the concepts could be carried over to the classroom. In one case we were able to have two students and two teachers work together. These two teachers voluntarily spent their preparation time in order to learn how to implement rating scales with their students. The two boys knew each other and were willing and able to participate together during most, but not all group sessions.

The rating scales were developed within the context of the "group." That is, although we had some ideas about what social situations and rating scales to develop, the actual scales were completed during our meetings. A set of statements coined "Understanding My Feelings" (see pages 42, 46, 50) were used to facilitate dialogue and the development of the rating scales. These worksheets lent themselves to cartooning or other drawings by the students. When creating scales, it is imperative to listen closely to what the students say and to use their language. If they don't have the necessary vocabulary to label what feelings or behaviors they are describing, or what others see them do, come up with the vocabulary together.

The boys actively participated in identifying the specific rating values and descriptions. Their teachers also gave their perceptions. The results were remarkably insightful. You will see that some of the rating scales are incomplete. They are works in progress, but are very close approximations of examples of the boys' hard work. The rating scales were developed when the students were fairly relaxed and in a comfortable environment, such as an office, so that we would not be distracted by interruptions or inadvertently be joined by other people. The teachers and students then worked on applying this information to other situations and environments.

"I'm 6'2", Strong as an Ox — So Can You Tell Me Why I'm Trembling?"

David was referred to the self-contained high school program after being expelled from his home high school. He had broken several windows in the school cafeteria and the glass entrance/exit door nearest to the cafeteria. As a result, he had been to juvenile court and was placed on probation.

David identified his behavior as self-defense. "It was like my head was going to explode because of all the noise and confusion in the cafeteria. It's always confusing, and today there was a food fight. I had to do something to make it stop, I was afraid my head was going to explode."

The rating scale that follows does not rate David's level of anger, but his fear. David told us he feels afraid when he is "confused" so when developing this scale, we discussed things that we were afraid of, and David drew pictures to help him understand his own fear.

Understanding My Feelings by David

Scared/Afraid

My word for this is:
trembling

This is how I look:

This is how my body feels:

This is what I do:
Hide.

This is what I say:
"I've got to get out of here!"

Things that David says make him "tremble":
"When I get confused."
"When it is loud and crowded."
"Catastrophes like tornadoes and earthquakes and war."

Name: <u>David</u>　　My <u>Scared/Afraid/Trembling</u> Scale

Rating	Looks/Sounds like	Feels like	Safe people can *help*/ I can try to
5	Wide-eyed, maybe screaming, and running, hitting.	I am going to explode if I don't do something.	I will need an adult to help me leave. Help!
4	Threaten others or bump them.	People are talking about me. I feel irritated, mad.	Close my mouth and hum. Squeeze my hands. Leave the room for a walk.
3	You can't tell I'm scared. Jaw clenched.	I shiver inside.	Write or draw about it. Close my eyes.
2	I still look normal.	My stomach gets a little queasy.	slow my breathing. Tell somebody safe how I feel.
1	Normal — you can't tell by looking at me.	I don't know, really.	Enjoy it!

I'm Afraid I'm Going to Lose Control

Adam reported that he had difficulty managing his anger. He has assaulted others, once with a tree branch. Another time he placed his hand around another person's neck as if to choke him. Both of these incidents happened while he was participating in an adapted recreation group social event, like a picnic or dance. Adam loves parties but is unable to manage his agitation, particularly if the event includes some sort of competition. In the above cases, Adam was highly distressed over losing a game. He hit the chaperone with the branch when he was told to sit out a game for using foul language, and he tried to choke his partner when they lost a game of tug-of-war.

Adam reported that the only time he was able to handle his anger during competitive games was when Lindsay, a staff person who used to supervise the adaptive recreation events, was there. Luckily, Lindsay was able to help create a scale for Adam. She said that she often noticed a change in Adam's body and facial expression prior to his loss of control. When she observed this change, she would prompt Adam to sit down and take a breather. This was not done as a punishment, but to help him regain his composure.

We developed a rating scale to illustrate how Adam "looks and acts" before he loses control to help increase his self-awareness. Adam's fear was that he did not have the skills to identify and manage his anxiety, and that consequently he would no longer be able to attend the social events.

The key to the success of this program was to inform all staff working the events that Adam was at risk when he was involved in anything of a competitive nature. All staff were given copies of the scale and directed to give Adam increased support near the end of game events. Adam himself was responsible for reviewing the scale prior to attending the events.

Although Adam continues to need support, he is beginning to learn to deal with the disappointment and frustration of losing. He recognizes some of his limitations and has opted not to play certain games if he is too worried about losing.

Understanding My Feelings by Adam

Scared/Afraid

My word for this is:
Shy

This is how I look:
Mean

This is how my body feels:
Sick

This is what I do:
Hide
Hit people

This is what I say:
Swear

"Quitting sports makes me afraid because I don't want to quit. I'm afraid I might lose control at a game or a practice or whatever."

– Adam

Name: <u>Adam</u>　　My <u>Scared/Afraid/Shy</u> Scale

Rating	Looks/Sounds like	Feels like	Safe people can *help*/I can *try* to
5	Swear Be mean Hit people Bite teeth tight	sick Stomach turns Head hurts See too much, eyes wide open	(Work in Progress)
4	Swear Yell loud	Feel sick	(Work in Progress)
3	Walk around room	Can't concen-trate Antsy	(Work in Progress)
2		My stomach starts turning over. A voice in my head tells me to do things.	Ask for or go for walk.
1	Put head down Hide Be quiet	Shy	Get reassurance from SAFE person.

"Take a Chill Pill, Sis"

Ben told his teacher that he said terrible things to his older sister and that he really didn't want to. He often engaged in verbal power struggles over doing chores, driving the family car, and so on. Frequently, interactions between Ben and his sister resulted in offensive language and even destruction of property. This is particularly troublesome because Ben's older sister, who attends a nearby community college, is often put in the position of looking out for him as his parents both work long hours and do not live together.

The following rating scale was developed when Ben's teacher shared with us that Ben was upset with himself over what he says and does when he is mad at his sister. He described a particular incident this way: "I had come home from working at my job for four hours. It was Friday. As soon as I walked in, my sister says, "You didn't do your chores. You have to before you can go out. And, I can't go out until you do!"

I told her, "That's not fair. I worked all day. Why don't you take a chill pill?" When she told me that I knew the rule about doing chores, I reminded her that last week she had let me go out before I had finished my chores.

This verbal exchange between Ben and his sister escalated to name calling on both sides, and eventually Ben left the house without finishing his chores. Before he left, he broke his sister's CD player and several CDs. He later came home and apologized, and offered to give his sister his CD player.

We asked Ben to fill out a feelings worksheet where he described the words he often uses, how his body feels, and how he looks when he is angry. The fact that he used swear words when filling in his rating scale was not judged as right or wrong, but simply as factual. (The use of these words was addressed later after Ben had gained some control of his destructive behavior.)

Besides rating his own anger, Ben also rated his sister's anger based on his perspective. Ben was limited in his ability to make a scale based on his sister's perspective, which is not surprising given the nature of his disability. Pulling the family into this situation proved helpful because Ben's sister and parents filled out scales based on their individual perspective. This information was extremely helpful to Ben, and it helped his family see how remorseful Ben was and how much he really wanted to work on his behavior. His parents also realized that Ben's sister needed more support in her interactions with Ben so that she didn't begin to resent spending time with him.

The process of change is often slow, and so it is in this case. Ben continues to struggle with his reactions to anger, but his destruction of property has decreased. He is working on role-playing possible frustrating situations and rehearsing reactions to help him cope better. He is also working on replacing swear words with other words so that he can eventually express his anger without intimidating or insulting his family, friends, boss, or other community members.

Understanding My Feelings by Ben

Mad/Angry

My word for this is:
Pissed off

This is how I look:
"How I feel I look, but I really wouldn't do it."

This is how my body feels:
"Like I will explode."

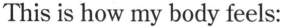

This is what I do:
"Throw stuff."

This is what I say:
*#!!@** #!@%/*##!!! ***#@//

Name: __Ben__   My __Angry/Pissed Off__ Scale

Rating	Looks/sounds like	Feels like	Safe people can *help*/I can *try* to
5	Swearing Breaking stuff Clenched teeth Wide-eyed	I have to break something Feels like I need to leave Like I will explode.	Help me leave. Take a walk with me.
4	Swearing	Mad.	Leave the room with permission to go to a safe place.
3	Not talking Pacing A little swearing	Upset.	Go get a drink.
2	Not happy Keeping to self Still interacting with others	?	Talk to a safe person. Use deep breathing.
1	None?	None?	Talk to a safe person. Use deep breathing.

Name: <u>Ben's Perspective</u> My <u>Big Sister's Anger</u> Scale

Rating	Looks/sounds like	Feels like	Safe people can help/I can try to
5	Bitching Yelling Screaming Throwing "You're grounded!"	Sick to stomach	
4	Ben says he doesn't know about "4" for his sister		
3	Ben says he doesn't know about "3" for his big sister		
2	Not talking Grumpy	Upset with another	Ben says he wishes his sister would leave.
1	Ben says he doesn't know about "1" for his sister		

Tell It Like It Is

The *Tell It Like It Is Scale* was developed for Richard, a ninth-grade student with ASD. Richard is partially mainstreamed but spends much of his day in a resource room. Richard often talks back to his teacher or the teacher aide when they ask him to do work tasks. His refusals include swearing. This usually invokes a reaction from the adult, which increases Richard's negative behavior. Richard is often asked to work in a timeout room as a result of these negative interactions. Frequently, his physical behavior escalates on the way to the timeout room (he throws chairs and desks).

The idea behind the scale was to take the control away from the negative behavior, create a program that was understandable to both Richard and the school staff, and teach Richard to recognize his rigidity and inflexibility. Richard was asked to rate himself three times a day (first thing in the morning, before lunch, and at 1:00 p.m.). The teacher wrote down the rating on his chart to remind himself of Richard's level of need. According to the ratings, Richard was set up at the group table (ratings 1 or 2), at his own desk (ratings 3 or 4), or in the timeout area (rating 5).

In addition, because verbal demands were typically met with resistance, the teachers began giving Richard written task lists (lists of 3-5 academic problems or tasks using the 1-5 terminology instead of verbally attending to any negative behavior). For example, when a student spoke to Richard and Richard yelled, "shut up!" the teacher told the other student that Richard was at a 3 at that moment and that he couldn't handle anybody talking to him. The teacher also reinforced Richard's ability to call a 3 a 3 when he was able to.

Richard later made a sign for his desk announcing to all which number he was at. This seemed to increase his ownership in the program and worked to help him communicate effectively with his classmates. The other students began enjoying rating themselves too, saying things like, "Bad night, I'm a 4 today."

Tell It Like It Is

 **5**   I need to leave!

_____

 **4**   I need some space

_____

 **3**   Please don't talk

_____

 **2**   I am a little nervous

_____

 **1**   I can handle this!

One Step Forward, Two Backward

Sam was in our classroom about six years ago, when he was 12 years old, and we've kept track of him over the years, as he has of us. Sam has ASD and obsessive compulsive disorder. He has trouble with basic academics like reading, writing and math.

The occasion of his 18th birthday was a period of significant regression for Sam. Recently, with the assistance of his current teacher, Sam called us. He was particularly worried about his need to move into an adult group home and had been hospitalized for a medication change. He told us that he wasn't doing well. In the Day and Habilitation Training Program he attended, "not doing well" manifested itself in excessive sleeping, disinterest in work and, of greatest significance, harassment and taunting of other vulnerable 18- to 21-year-old students. Sam said he could not stop himself from the serious taunting and was worried about it. He also told us that he was not being physically aggressive.

Since we do not work at Sam's program or with him directly any more, this was a "create a rating scale right now" kind of a deal. This is the beauty of these scales. You can put them together methodically and polish them up or, as in this case, you can put one together on the fly. Sam's teacher had called us the day before, stating that Sam was not doing well. We were able to meet with Sam at his training program the next morning shortly after the start of his day. When we arrived, Sam was lying with a blanket under the sink in the nurse's office. We sat on the floor next to him, as did his teacher. It was important that the teacher was there as the rating scale would have to be polished up by Sam's teacher and others at his program since we would not be able to return to the site except to check in.

We wanted Sam and his teacher to identify whom he considered "safe people" at his program (people whom Sam perceives as understanding his disability and behavior) and "safe places" (places identified by Sam and the staff as places he can go to get away when he feels he may be unable to manage taunting in his current environment). All the significant people in Sam's life need to know who the safe people are and where the safe places are. Communication with team and family members is essential and should occur via a team meeting, phone calls, e-mail, or by whatever means the team members communicate with each other.

The following two scales were developed with Sam's input along with that of his teacher, right there in the nurse's office. The teacher agreed to work with Sam once a day to role-play, rehearse, and study the scales.

Sam and his teacher practiced what to do when Sam feels he is reaching a 3 on either scale. A 3 on the *What Am I Saying Scale* would indicate that it is time to find a safe place, away from people, to reduce the possibility of negative interactions and further escalation. A 3 on the *Monitoring My Anxiety Level Scale* would indicate that Sam needs help from a safe person so someone can assist him in regulating his anxiety. Sam needs an adult nearby when he is feeling anxious, which is also a time he is afraid of losing control and does not want to be left alone.

Not only did Sam learn to control his verbal taunting, but a year later he got a job doing janitorial work at a school program for children with severe cognitive disorders – something that would not have been possible if he had not learned to control his behavior with support from others.

Monitoring My Anxiety Level
A Rating Scale for Sam

 Forget it. My self-control is zero.
I need an advocate.

_____

 It is pretty hard for me to control myself. I'll
need somebody safe with me or a way out in
a hurry.

_____

 I'm okay. But I would like somebody
nearby to support me.

_____

 I'm cool.

_____

 No problem. I'm in complete control
for at least ___ minutes. I'll even be
able to help someone else.

What Am I Saying?
A Rating Scale for Sam

Taunting (for example, "I could kill you."
"Go over and spit on the teacher.")
[I need help.]

Negative interactions (for example, "I'm not
going to do the work." "I hate this place."
"Quit following me around.")

Short or no interactions, neutral.
[Give me my space.]

"Common" interactions (exchanging information
about the weekend, asking what's for lunch,
saying "hi.") [I'm fine.]

Positive interactions (initiated, "How are you?"
"I'm glad I'm here." "You look great!)
[I'm upbeat. I could help somebody else.]

References

Asperger, H. (1944). Die 'Autistichen Psychopathen' im Kindersalter. *Archiv für Psychiatrie und Nervenkrankheiten, 117*, 76-136.

Gray, C. (1995). *Social stories unlimited: Social stories and comic strip conversations.* Jenison, MI: Jenison Public Schools.

Kanner, L. (1943). Autistic disturbances of affective contact. *Nervous Child, 2*, 227-250.

Appendix

We have added three more scale ideas and two blank scales for you to try. Remember that every student and every situation is different. A given student's problem may not fit neatly onto one of our scales. If this is the case, remember the concepts underlying the use of the scale (break the behavior down and make it visual), and you will be able to create your own incredible scales.

Group Check-In

We use this to start the Social Understanding groups we hold. Each person (including adults) rates himself or herself as 1-5 when coming to group. We have explained to students and teachers that if students rate themselves at a 1, they don't have to stay. Believe it or not, we have never had anybody rate himself at a 1! If participants rate themselves at a 2 they stay, but they don't have to participate. This strategy has worked in groups with students with emotional/behavioral disorders as well as with Asperger Syndrome and autism.

The Stress Scale

We have used this scale when interviewing students as a part of a functional behavior assessment to identify situations they perceive as particularly stressful. This is a good tool to help set up an environmentally modified program. The scale also lends itself to a discussion of supports students feel they need in order to be successful.

The High-Low Scale

We used this scale in a social skills group at an elementary school. We made a big scale and posted it on the wall, and then used a moveable arrow to point to different numbers on the scale (1= being relaxed and 5=out of control). Then we asked the students to practice looking like a 1, 2, 3, 4 or 5. We also used sticky notes on the chart to represent thinking bubbles indicating what other people might think when we act in certain ways.

Blank Scales

The blank scales on pages 69 and 71 are two of our most popular versions of the scale (if a scale can be popular). We have modified the scales to fit many different situations, but these two prototypes have been the most useful.

Visual Prompts

Finally, we have included a page of small scales that can be laminated, cut out, and used to visually prompt a child or student when a specific problem arises. When prompting the student, point to the number you want him or her to be at rather than where the student currently is. This seems to work best and prompts the person in the direction you want her to go rather than where you don't want her to be. We wear our small scales around our necks with our staff ID tags. Parents have put them in the visor in the car to prompt car-riding behavior, or in their wallet to pull out when they are in the community.

As much as we love our little 5-point scale, we know that it can only be a part of a total plan to support individuals with ASD. We hope you find the concept helpful in your efforts to teach positive behavior change to your students and children.

Group Check-In

 **5** I am really glad to be here. I will participate and I may even be able to help others.

 **4** I am glad to be here and I will participate.

 **3** I'm here. I might or might not participate.

 **2** I'm here. I will not participate but I will not disrupt.

 **1** I will not participate and I may disrupt if I have to stay.

The Stress Scale

 **5**   I could lose control

_____

 **4**   Can really upset me

_____

 **3**   Makes me nervous

_____

 **2**   Bugs me

_____

 **1**   Never bothers me

The High-Low Scale

Practice shifting between numbers. How do they look? How do they feel?
What does your face feel like?

High

5

4

3

2

1

Low

That person is scary!

I like to sit near you.

OK	Not OK	Topic:_____
		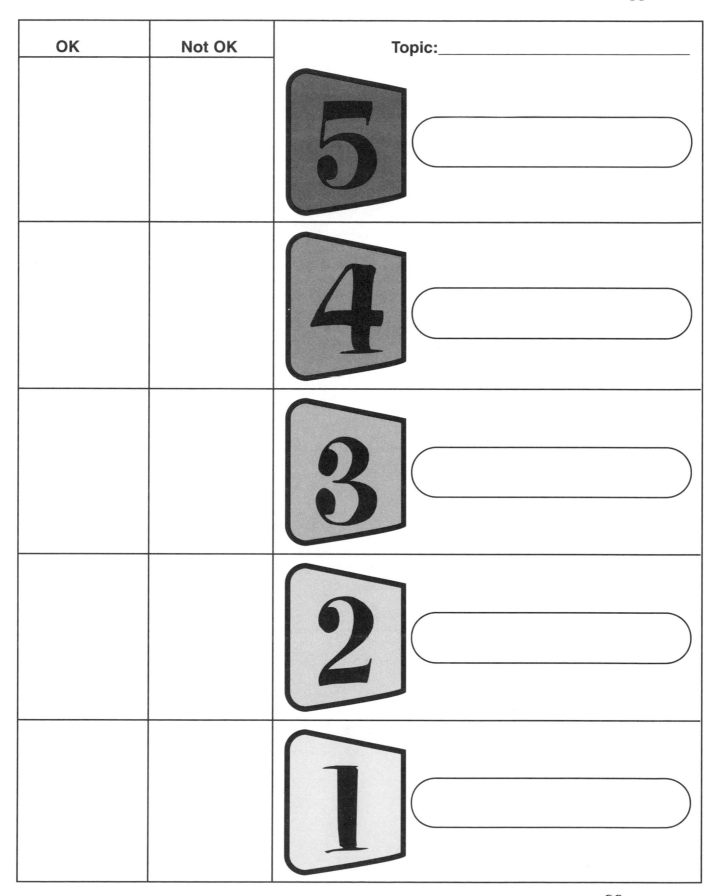

Name: _____ My _____ Scale

Rating	Looks like	Feels like	I can *try* to
5			
4			
3			
2			
1			

Visual Prompts
Tear off and carry with you.

5	5	5	5
4	4	4	4
3	3	3	3
2	2	2	2
1	1	1	1
5	5	5	5
4	4	4	4
3	3	3	3
2	2	2	2
1	1	1	1